sidelines
MAX LOMAS

Dedication

Vernon Hoffman was born in South Africa with multiracial legacies that he refused to compartmentalise as he also rejected splitting art and life. He migrated to Australia, where he taught English, enthusing his students, colleagues and this writer with ebullience and wit.

Sidelines
ISBN: 978 1 7610990 8 3
Copyright © text Max Lomas 2025
Cover design by Graham Davidson

First published 2025 by
Ginninderra Press
PO Box 2 Bentleigh 3204
ginninderrapress.com.au

Contents

Preface	7
meditation	9
Murray River Weekend	10
fragments	11
Birthday Poem	12
Ken Reading	13
Traducción	14
Kazuko reading	16
Man of Straw	17
of friends divorcing	19
Scene Change	20
Expatriate Patriot	21
Euclid	22
sexual politics	24
Sensitive Plant	25
Colonial History	26
Postgraduate Interlude	28
During wind and rain	29
Still Life: Hawai'i	30
Commentary	34
The Greening of Adelaide	35
Labour History	36
Reverie	37
For Frank	38
Rakhi for Raji	40
Haphazard	41
For Auden and Cohorts	42
A Lay for Modern Poets	44
Once around the block	46

The first real squirrel	48
Parallax Error	50
Eventually	51
Bemused	52
First Flight Home	54
Time to go	55
Tidings of Comfort and Joy	59
Wet season nocturnes	60
Banana Leaf	62
haiku moods	63
Escalation (A Reagan/Gaddafi remonstrance)	64
Caesura	66
Memo	67
Magical realism	69
'Killer Litter' (HDB, Singapore)	70
Old Lag	72
Ulysses returned	73
Angry every day	76
Displacement	77
A Sceptic's Credo	82
Continuity	83
Critical Response	84
What bird is that?	86
Portrait of the camel as Australian	87
Fremantle Reading	88
Extrapolation	89
An Investment	90
Crumbs from an Australian Table	91
Koha	92
Idiom in Auckland	94
St Francis Church, Cochin	95
Kanyakumari	98

Private Tuition	100
Brett and Jodi un-Donne	101
Separation Blues	102
Overseas Conference	104
Pucker up	106
At the Airport, Seattle	107
Another damn elegy	108
the long-term car park	111
starting over	112
Gold room #3, Hakoah Club	114
Conferencing, Hyderabad	115
Sonnet XXXX	116
Country, and Western	117
while you sleep	118
In Anticipation	119
Rumi to Shahms	120
Sequel	122
Stone Poem	123
The Rubbayyat of Max	125
After Rumi	126
On not meeting the great poet	127
Secular landscape	128
Towing	130
Deb's place, Calcutta	132
Slogans for Senators	133
Nature	134
Nicosia by the wall	135
Two Sonnets for Syd	136
Night sweats	138
Requiem	139
Epitaph for Chas	140
DOA	142

To the Makers	143
Views from home	144
Amnesia/Scission	145
Developments	146
Language lessons (lyrics for a ballad)	147

Preface

This collection is made up of occasional verse, which is to say poems written only occasionally. They make no claim on merit as 'high art' from someone centrally engaged in questions of literary craft except in so far as they try to follow Ezra Pound's nostrum that a poem should be an appropriate mix of thought, music and image. The poems arise from personal experience, situations, feelings, scenes, but self-indulgence is given (I hope) some generalising distance by edits to provide shape and measure, edits that with any luck add a bit of concision and depth. I hope the result is accessible, even enjoyable, to others. What appear here are selected from the jottings of a lifetime and appear in chronological order of their creation.

meditation

1970/86

Words
flow on
                      spread out
    so
splashes in a stream.
Water
is clouded by urgency,
effort.
Ripples
                stilled
    so
pebbles shine
clear through
crystal vapour.

Now and then
a flash
        of rainbow.

Murray River Weekend

1975

Cliffs of chalk and ochre, sun-dried
slabs of orange and grey
gnawed at by brown water
and white, foaming men
spraying V8 virility
at the clay and stone.

They roar at towering past,
call back-up from
a flood of present and
the ceaseless lapping future.

Thrust is turned echoing aside
by the age of elements;
nature's hourglass in bronze and gold
cuts the nylon link of man and motor,
smoothes over the presumptuous wake,
enfolding a dying curve of ski
in sibilant diminuendo.

Stillness.

fragments

1975/86

i

The philosopher's stone has dragged
its human lode into a molten
gold Sargasso. And Cristóbal is
as blind as Galileo.
The fountain of youth spouts
samples from a Jap factory in Brazil
for senile painted savages
on their fourth voyage
circumnavigating the globe.

ii

Prospero, Duke of Milan,
as a statesman was rather a ham;
philosophical study made
his politics muddy –
Milano, Gottamo…
Goddamn,
the Three Wise Men
went to sea in a bowl;
if it had been stronger,
the Christ child
would never have hanged. Still,
he's have copped it somehow,
and Hieronymus
would have found other knives
to crack eggs with.

Birthday Poem

1976/1986

We forget old Time, but back he always comes,
dressed as a rag-and-bone man, stumbling with
the ruthless bonhomie of a drunkard against
events; a bemused pause to contemplate
sadly the ruins of his passage, then
he shakes his head and shuffles past. Too late
we brace ourselves to meet his bleary eye,
his rolling gait. A moment's hesitation
and we smile, horror-struck, confronted by
the undeniable, embarrassing relation.

But here tonight there's no embarrassment,
and riches, health, love, fortune and good wine
will fortify us as we, for the moment,
stop him in his tracks, friends revelling with Time.

Ken Reading

1978/83/86

In the pauses, mind
                  slips away
                              down
the back staircase
of
      your
              ageing
                        tongue.

There,
diffident mirth
finds shadows grown
compelling
sombre, feels
the dark swarm moving
sounds drawn
from the horde
of glowing memory.

Suddenly in silence
old passions pursued
                  ignite
        flare golden,
and words light up again
the listening heart.

Traducción

1978–9

Me dicen que, como siempre, hay dos modos:
el uno es de cobre y el otro, plata.
Recobrando palabra por palabra
el sentido, se esfuerza a hallar el todo.

El Segundo, dicen, tiene más logro:
se puede sacar del poema el alma
y, con su espíritu, ganar la palma,
creando el fuente sin cavar el pozo.

Pero, para poner en otro sitio
un edificio, se descubre su planta
demoliéndolo con guantes de seda;

y sin una montaña de granito
no tendríamos ningún diamante,
ni de eso la luz brillante que queda.
They always say there are two methods:

one copper, the other silver.
Collecting the meaning word
by word, one tries for the whole.

The second, they say, works better;
You extract the poem's soul and, fired
by its spirit, grab the prize
without running the race.

But to shift a building from one place
to another, you must check the floor-plan
and demolish anything with kid gloves.

If there were no granite mountains
there would be no diamonds
nor the brilliance they leave behind.

Kazuko reading
1980/86/06

Black sheen of hair
fall
        leap
of voice
        turns
wandering
Ulysses
oriental to her siren
        jazz
Coltrane screaming to
an underground
        didgeridoo
and where is
        home?

Man of Straw
1976/86

Couch grass, forked
and forking brother to
the burrowing worm,
Lucifer among my garden's angels,
I turn the seasons over
in pursuit of you.

Yours are stealthy ways,
white veins and yellow tendons
threading on an eyeless needle,
knotted, brittle yarn of labyrinths
arthritic, tangled around stones,
bones of the years' detritus.

No dramatic mandrake,
your death-cry
is a dry chuckle.
Like the worm you seem
to have the knack of
self-regeneration, so that
as I tear my fingernails
cracking the clay matrix
from your bronze roots,
I'm mocked by shreds of
hollow shells and broken shoots.
The earth now reddening in my hands
will afterwards put on a new green skin.

And as I pile your dried remains
and pace a magic circle round your pyre,
I hear the spluttering in the flames
and feel the binding sinews reaching out,
thin fingers digging at my grave.

# of friends divorcing

1979/81/86

The wonders of the world are no more with us.
The Gardens hung in a withering sun;
Zeus's etched marble does not impress,
and the Colossus enjoys a diminished stature.

No one today is awe-struck
at a mausoleum, now
the Lighthouse flame's ambiguous
in the Library's burning glow.

As for the Pyramids, the stones
have questioned where their meaning
lies, have quietly torn away,
fretted into drab atoms.

Well, you know how it is
watching others suffer:
grief puts up 'No Trespassers'
and what can you say?
No real cases seem relevant
or even compelling – take ours:
no wonder for the history books,
but we get by, even
when we don't get along.

And I, from all desolation,
cannot preach an easy solace
of restored structures, can bear
faint witness only to the
grandeur of solid form.

Scene Change

1981

'All the world's a stage,' says the Bard, and so
it is: we rage and weep, contend with gods
in one form or another, make heroes
and villains out of mere acquaintances,
marry, murder, bestow rule, use rod
and, at the prompting of some low sentence,
we die. It's so neat; what more could you ask?
A smile or a grimace – both serve as a mask.

But in my acts the curtain keeps falling
at the wrong time. Despite my rehearsals
the lines are strange, the prompt always stalling,
and props are never in the expected spot;
director's commands suffer reversals –
it's not theatre; but I do suspect a plot.

Expatriate Patriot
1981/1986

It depends a bit on where you go,
I guess, and who you know,
but you'll meet blokes here with
all the badges of their nationhood
ablaze on every bag, emblazoned
in each word and gesture, who – it's queer –
at home would never, even in their sleep,
dream once of waving their country's flag.

You'll find these types in two mobs
mostly, one'll say their homeland's
'best of all but bloody costly',
the other that it's
'not the worst, but cheap.'

And both agree you'll tend to find
that travel, 'weeell, it broadens the mind',
but being abroad is a drag.

Euclid
1982

Your mental exercises –
elegant demonstrations
of the axiomatic:

'Such beautiful theorems,' said
the headmaster, misty-eyed,
the square on the hypotenuse
of his nose pointing
to the neatly squared ceiling.

Behind his back, across the room,
a triangle – isosceles –
winged an almost perfect circle
(circumference of which times twice
the radius by three point one,
add whatever infinitum –
fascinating things,
numbers)
propelled by one of the asses
cut off by your bridge.

I suppose there was inherent
satisfaction, matching ideas
to lines, angles –
and planes.

Now that ass
bucks about
in a metal colossus
with your name up front,
helps gouge
lines and spirals deep
into the earth's face;

and the top of the class
is into ballistics.

To prove this is not so
assume it isn't
and show that to be
impossible.
QED.

sexual politics

1982

Last month I drank
through an evening full
of wry poems about
divorce
full of self
congratulation:
felt amazed our marriage
had survived
so long.

Tonight, cast loose,
a lone party
intoxicated,
one suntanned lady
in whose dark-lined eyes,
black wild-ruffed hair,
one could weave
fantasies
says, 'Left your wife
and kids
at home again?'

Sensitive Plant

1982

It was almost hidden by the high-rise, down
along the concrete, reaching over
to the giveaway tropic shanty piled
around with junk and backyard jungle –

the fragile green and darkly edged
purple delicate acacia fronds:
mimosa pudica. Fingers stretched,
a touch, hesitant, instinctive folding in.

Finding it raised pleasant memories
of other tropic places, adolescent
sun-baked drenched green and dusty
rambles: solitude in bustling times.

More for joy of sharing reconnections,
I called my son to please his curiosity,
and we poked about with glee amongst
the straggled couch and tangled vine.

Shrinking in quietly, softly closing
the door, next day he told me, weeping,
the local kids were teasing him
for not knowing how to play their games.

Colonial History

1983

It was bliss
then,
strolling under rows of waving fronds
along the endless lapping shore.

Hard to think
that idle
native
neither fortunate nor
lazy, but
dying
slowly
of a cancered mouth.

And hard
to learn
that tropic palms
were forced
plantings
to raise a
foreign government tax.

Walking home from school,
four miles alone
of sun and quiet dust,
dropping
a few words
of proudly possessed
vernacular
like alms
upon dark smiling faces,
protected
by youth,
vulnerable
white skin,
and its long history
or reprisals.

Hard, now,
to feel
innocence:
to know
then
it was blind.

Postgraduate Interlude

1983

Outside
two wagtails feint,
edging quick about
an unseen centre,
flit,
black
on white cloud,
blue field of air.

Across the room
a slanting winter sun
picks out sharp the edges
of my library, bright
rectitude of spines
leaning in to shade
rows still to read.

During wind and rain
1983

Outside,
the rush and thrash of frantic wind.
My half-face in the dark pane.

Plants stumble, clutch each other,
forms surfacing from shadow.

Windows sound in their frames.
A shiver of body
ghosts down my side.

Still Life: Hawai'i

1983

i

Last seen   hand raised against
the grey sky shining
line of black lava plain
rock   you seem
a silent exclamation
in your red dress,
Ariadne.

Disaster should follow,
and wind chorus its
threnody around her
sea of grief.
                    Oh
Earthshaker, swallow me!

Where are the gods,
when I never took
one photo in respect
of the ruined temple?

ii

Captured   gazing
from house beyond
the brown window framing
heights of sepia mountain ridges
ivory   arms
a rigid supplication,
your coast half flowers
in the glass.

Rescue should follow,
and ageing stand there
open-mouthed on her
tedious isle.
                       Yet Oh
Great Warrior, come for me!

Why didn't I know
it could not be right
the minute I saw him
coming up from the sea?

iii

That day   pausing
side by side amidst
the rainbow dripping
through indigo leaf vaults
gold   the fish
rising like islands
in your dark pool;
you in garlands.

Then is black sorrow,
and rain threads a
labyrinth in her
midnight hair.
                     Oh
Fisherman, cut your hook!

How did he go
when we'd wrapped rock
in leaf together, made
offering at the shrine?

iv

There was no black storm
that tossed away your craft.
Slow lichen patterns
silver green the lava stones.

This piece arises from a dream picture of a friend in distress. It seeks to capture a quality of ritual drama from Classical tragedy in allusions to Hawaiian beliefs.

The goddess Pele commands volcanic eruptions and is associated with a deluge myth. She is popularly thought to stand by the Pali highway, hitching rides in a red dress.

Old temple sites are still considered sacred. Ancestral spirits are honoured by leaving one of the many lava stones of the walls wrapped in a ti leaf. It is bad luck to remove stones from such a site and photographs are sometimes reported not to work because of the currents of power at these locations.

Half-flowers symbolise the sundered love of a princess for a commoner. One form of the plant producing semicircular blossoms grows only on the coast, another only in the mountains.

The rainbow is a favourite symbol on Oahu.

Hawaiians traditionally farmed fish in large rock ponds. The fisherman is a reference to the demi-god Maui. Allusion to Japanese-Hawaiian rock gardens and pools for koi (carp) is also made.

Commentary
1983

Have you observed how
from that time onwards
        it is as though
every piece is framed
by something in the margin
        some hidden centre
a ritual tribute
separate presence
        shakes the passions
other than the story
absently containing
        turbulations of text
end included?

The Greening of Adelaide
1983

In the better suburbs
corridors of trees
stand quiet in place
of natural order.

Trunks open and shut
for drives to sleep,
ritual linking of
one block to another,
beside the bottles
of wine and other
weekly leavings.

Along the gutters
scuttering husks
of plane and kurrajong,
jacaranda and
the squawk of the grey
wattlebird rattle
a longing for the
tortuous noise, the
sweaty oppression
of teeming jungle.

Labour History

1983

On the faster back roads to work
we'd pass the cornered yarding
of the old glue factory: grey
splintered posts and rails, dust, a herd
of brumbies and old nags, black ramps
and angled red metal – lead and rust;
a hot stench like mouldy sugar-bags.

Now it's 'super glue'; the horses,
doubly obsolete, have gone,
the sheds are on the scrap heap
and the workers, all
put out to pasture,
know what it means
to be really
knackered.

Reverie

1983/86

Lost:
one guitar.

Schoolrooms of black
necks bulging red and
green felt bellies;

a tool shed of banjos,
squat tubas and rubber
boots, bassoons,
cardboard coffins
in wheelbarrows.

Eye's corner knew:
there stood the real case.
but mind refused,
fossicked doggedly on
through debris.

Distracted,
that day
strayed.

For Frank

1983

Old man
you've done it
all, seen it
all and, if not,
read of it, and
now
you're rich with
time and
words to
tell it
all.

But time
for you is
cheap, words are
cheap, and
how
poor you've
soon become.

Your capital devalues and
coins tarnish with use:
the more you spend
the less change there is.

Old man,
I'm grateful
for your time,
for the words.
But leave
some
for your testament.
I will not use
your words,
I cannot spend
your time.

Grant me
leave
to do and see and
feel and read
and spend and speak for
myself.

Rakhi for Raji
1984

Sitting at a window
again on the twelfth floor,
I remember
watching the clarity
of light glaze the
crisp greenery, and you
remarked I wrote of mountains
while your mind
moved always seaward.

How long since we were talking?

Now you've landed up
in waves of Mysore trees, red soil,
while I, from home to work
face daily the ocean's spread brilliance.

Somewhere between, think of a line;
on this turns the balance
of a friendship.

Haphazard

1984

And this is the friend with the car
I was waiting for, who couldn't get through
to tell me he'd come later;
here too, is the phone out of order
which is the reason I was waiting
in incipient rain and failing light
with some tutorial reading to kill time
and a banana to delay hunger.

Here is the page of the book with the stain
of the peel that remained
when the car arrived, urgently late,
leaving me no chance
to dispose of it properly.

And this is the other friend, the one
we were meeting at the airport,
whose plane was delayed, for which reason
I was outside with Conrad,
the dusk, and a banana skin.

And here is the poem
that slipped out, haphazard,
from the stain of a banana skin,
a book, late friends,
and waiting.

For Auden and Cohorts
(or 'Oh shit, here's another one…')
1984

Small wonder
that poets are such pricks;
they practise an arrogant art…

form that batters sense
and bludgeons the mind with
ROMAN UPPER CASE CONCERNS
and the fucking buffets of outrageous speech
preaching the commitments
of a various conversion/

Poems that insinuate a Need
to spend a Lifetime following their Lead.

The epic work dumped midway in our path
vaunting by its bulk we ought not look
at other works, contemporary or past

of its kind, or even any other book;
but from its pages glean sufficient craft
and wisdom upon which to hook
a compleat educacioun.

And more imposing still
(empty tenement blocks with graffitied walls
and the one footfall in the shadow of noon –
there, by the trash cans in the back lot)
are the private lines
inviting as you skim the page to
linger
        coffee grounds
images
        slopping through the filter
ponder the dark rose
        at the bottom of the pot
of hidden meaning
        /s
reaching out the hand of artifice
to arrest time itself and hold
self and other in
        a dreaming garden
confined
        in walls of conceit
wide as the world.

A Lay for Modern Poets

1984

The carriages are all
illuminated texts,
metal volumes of some
Book of Hours for
contemporary devotees.

The reading for today
is, 'Go to work
on an egg.'

Some say that the egg
      is the shuttle
      by which we
           are all
      transported
from one station
to new states beyond.

      For
           others,
      the chicken
           is a vehicle
through which eggs
      drive more
           eggs.

Is this text a shell

in which readers scramble
for private destinations?
Am I a vain carrier
of literary germinations?
Or are poets just eggs –
destined to be cracked?

Only a train
of thought.

Once around the block
1984

The passionate topography of cities:
lava-flows of asphalt, pitted
craters of black gravel
crumbling ragged wave
convolutions, all highlighted
in knife-edge darkness and peaks of gold
by the shadows of a late sun;

the fault-lines of techtonic plates
thrusting upwards from concrete paving;
rift valleys where the council
has just laid a drain;

how corners catch a flood of debris –
emerald deposits of glass shard,
steel fragments
(heel tips, nuts and washers, burnished
silver, paperclips), a copper coin,
the gray matt of self-tappers,
a rubber bush or two, cracked
and whitening around the edges –

the gutter-bound lateral moraine

of a day's waste and the street's
glacial dawn sweeper – all
the erosion of industry
mapped in the eye of the stranger,
the walker at evening, the
crazed beggar on the corner, all
amazed at the fervent beauty
of a city.

The first real squirrel

1984 New York

Dodging the sun's heat and the beat
of the ghetto-blaster enthroned
on the centre of the dry fountain,
I sidestep as matter-of-factly as possible
the man at the Arch hurling himself
after his own Frisbee.
Avoiding the eye of the gliding figure
selling 'Smoke. Smoke' in smooth sotto voce,
step into the shadows
of the park and stop
as something dips a gentle course
across my path – a pigeon
with four legs and – no,
Good lord, a squirrel!

Pause for recognition of the fact;
the pert, red mischief-makers from a world away
of illustrated childhood do not fit
this dun and grizzled-silver rodent
dragging its brush flat down.
Only a quick nibbling at the forepaws
and the alert flashing of a dark eye
offsets the anonymity of the public animal
going privately about its livelihood.
How commonplace things seem in their own setting.

You wouldn't believe it
when I told the detail from a day
wandering the backstreets of your city's village.
And suddenly we talked
in foreign beastly tongues
of kangaroos and emus,
beaver, bear.

But your eyes brought back the wonderment
of new encounters, and now
memories are retouched
with shining spontaneity;
I think how wondrous little
we know each other's worlds,
how well we are accommodated in them
when we enter caring.

Parallax Error
1984

Life's full of surprises
so often not more
than chance
miscalculations –
lips pursing as the hand
extends towards you;
the kiss askew on your mouth
when you'd been heading
for a friendly cheek.

Small failures
of judgement, haphazard
sentimentalities of meeting
and departure become
illuminating moments,
lasting mortifications.

These are such stuff
as dreams are made on.

Eventually
1984

Wailing   out
their   grief
against   me
women
have come and
gone
I am
no use
they   cry
at   my   silence.

What
is there to say?

It   takes
time.

I am
a   slow
learner.

Bemused

1984 Manoa

Escaping television and
the mechanical child
on the piano in the next house,
I take my back-issue literature
outside into the sun.

But today everything
is in motion.
The bright hillside rears
green-flecked and driven.
Tree-tops tug and plunge at their moorings
and roofs ride like flotsam
washed with sheets of gusting air.

Cloud-spray whiteness stings the eyes;
the whole island coruscates with wind.

Pages fluster, once, twice
are swept away,
picked spare.
Mind is body, body mind –
a lean quicksilver fusion,
bare enthusiasm sharp-edged
as a blast of ozone.

Of a sudden all loyalties
and loves of reason snap.
Passions cast loose, impetuous
to race before a ferment of light,
sails set tight and high to chase
a sapphire dazzlement of eyes.

First Flight Home
1984

Here again everything
is distance, flat lines and quiet;
even the rays of light come down
wavering, horizontal.
The clouds are banked away
like new wool, scoured and carded fine;
a breeze insinuates itself
along a wire fence.

The fresh-cut row of forest
sliced open like a midnight wheat field,
a strip of white sand,
silver water flats,
lacings of tractor tyres in black mud –
all softened in blue smoke-drifts
from flattened timber
sullenly burning.

Two things stand out from this:
a new and underutilised airport
asserts its completion
in spare verticals of metal;

and against tinted windows,
with muted slaps
a tiny kingfisher flashes
its frenzy, turning,
turning.

Time to go
1985 Honolulu

i

This morning, quietly sitting out
a cup of coffee, another
chapter of an obscure novel, idle
customary banter with the waitress:
'Stir your dark roast today, honey?'
'What d'you get
mixing Kenya and Kona?
Answer: an F
in geography.'

I look up, and suddenly
there, the mountains
set against the window,
dark translucency
grinding emerald bright
edges on the glass.

ii

The squatter's shack, for years suspended,
a brown challenge of dark angles
amongst the hillside brush,
is a ripped white open half
of sprawling scrap matchwood
on the slide.

The mad lady I used to meet
muttering imprecations in Hawaiian
five times about the city in a day,
has changed her beat.
And the man of the four rustling bags
and twenty kinds of dark glasses
now condescends a friendly chat
to make me feel at home.

iii

Yesterday I got away,
got on my bike and rode
for sixty miles. A break;
and coming at me up the street –
heads bent on cones of rainbow ice,
a free arm distractedly waving –
two fellow workers from the office.

There's no getting away from it;
all the laws are soon made evident:
the local beauty basking in the two-piece
is with the muscle out there in that canoe;
attractive tourists move in custody
of plainly overweight companions
(symbiosis of protective chatter and
vicarious excitement).
Tomorrow's waves will fall,
will seem to fall, will leave
impressions of falling
just like today's.

iv

White pigeons fluttering on the beach
invoke an absence of raucous gulls.
The mynahs have been away too long,
leaving only the indifferent foraging
of servile crawling flocks of small gray doves.
Summer drought is turning tropic lawns
the straw colours of my memories,
and last night I saw clearly
the uncompromising black and white
of two magpies in a dry tree,
filling the smoked expanse of mauve dusk
with rippling fugal melodies.

Tidings of Comfort and Joy
1985

Writers and critics of the world give ear;
the humanities are now demonstrably
central to technological progress.
We need no longer feel an undue fear;
the pen really is mightier than the sword.

Neither, dearly beloved, let us kid ourselves.
The millennium will be ushered in
by an Armageddon of scriptural terrorists
arguing fundamentally the status
of the text, battling fiercely fine points
on correct interpretations of the word.

Wet season nocturnes

1985 Singapore

i

rain   a solid wall outside
sheer leaden noise   at times
translucent silver   glazed
by sheeted lightning;

                        here

on the second storey
we are illuminated

                        clean

bodies

                        suspended

in a cubicle of air.

ii

Here, and at this time of year
you do not waft to dreams
on dry silence;
sleep is drilled into you
in mechanic symphony –

the insects' insistent hysteric crescendo;
dry midnight leaves fall intermittent, flat;
a splatter of rain on the dark leaf-scaled grass;

and concerted groanings
from a distant speedway:
the tuning up of a hundred frogs
and toads of assorted formulae,
all droning wildly,
drunk on the fumes
of a day's rain.

Banana Leaf

1985

Slender inverted cone
of upright lucent green
unfurls slow and formal
as a bright oriental banner.

So fresh as yet it is
without a character,
luminous blazon
of promised coming.

Stiff ribbed silk
holds sway above
tatters of drooping flags:
yesterday's dynasties.

It heralds again the
golden court, a cluster
of beauty and good taste
that will last forever.

haiku moods

1985

i

bright sun and blue bay;
fingerlings of light leaping,
the sea spawns silver.

ii

bodies still slow sigh,
fretful tugs tense at the sheet;
echoes not speaking.

iii

racing on the road
'Out of my way, you fuckwit!'
exhaust enraged heart.

Escalation (A Reagan/Gaddafi remonstrance)

1986

Falling out
takes two.

All it takes
is two
and some pride.

All it takes
is two
and pride
and a gun.

All it takes
is two
and pride,
some rhetoric,
and a gun.

All it takes
is two
and pride
and rhetoric,
religion,
and guns.

All it takes
is two,
some pride,
rhetoric,
religion,
or skin,
and guns.

All it takes
is two
and pride
and rhetoric,
religion
or skin,
and followers,
and guns
and guns
and guns.

And the fallout begins
with just
two.

Caesura

1986

Dodging the latticed shadows
of two naked lights, eyes
blink over thirty hurried hands,
pen flicks through brainwaves
grappling to understand
how lit. crit. can be so
unpractical, prosaic, perverse –

all at once –
nothing.

An insect
slicing through atmospheres
on sonic overdrive,
cuts its rockets.

Freed
of an unnoticed
adversary,
mind
floats loose
in darkness,
silence.

Memo

1984/1986

(in response to one about Hawaiian shirts being inappropriate dress for teaching)

i

When teaching D.H. Lawrence on the dead weight
of convention and bureaucracy,
is it appropriate to be bound neck and knee
by codes of the respectably out-of-date,
the ghostly freight of someone else's training,
or is it rank hypocrisy?

ii

And what about this image we should all strive to maintain?

May our accoutrements convey that love of learning
is a dowdy show, respectable, but still a fashion,
that pursuit of knowledge fits the habits of privilege,
that passion has no place in the caparison of truth?

Let's not kid ourselves about the trappings of academe:
nobility is not essential to computer work,
there's nothing dignified about dissecting rats,
and little that is holy in analysing the stats
of voting patterns. Nor do we need genteel attire
to experience with the poets that we all expire.

Ought we in our vestments signify that scholarship
is merely one more carriage on a sordid gravy train –
that those with wealth and wit to stick it long enough to pass
will win the tickets they already have to ride first class?

iii

Let us now turn to the letter
of the law, the code of better
conduct, and neatly dress ourselves
in definitions, take from the dusty shelves

some properly ruled conditions, What
for instance, makes a shirt 'Hawaiian'?
Is its being made or got
within the sound of palm-trees sighing

and the waves of Waikiki the thing
that counts (and what shirts do they wear
to teach 'appropriately' over there?)?
Or is it that a shirt should cling

instead of being a floral bag
to raise offensive hue and cry
by its pattern or its tag
or the assault of colours on the eye?

Perhaps it's inappropriately tropic
to wear such for an academic topic;
but should we make, as something better,
our presence drab, our clothes a fetter?

Magical realism
1986

Yesterday I met a man
trades in commodities –
mostly futures, he says
it's a game where you try
to out-guess the others.
None of them see anything
of the stuff they deal in
– not a coffee bean, not
a solitary grain of
silicon.
         He used to be
a sea-captain, is now
building a catamaran
to be provisioned with
hydroponic tomatoes:
his hedge against
the future.

'Killer Litter' (HDB, Singapore)

1986

This is a clean city,
one of the tidiest in Asia.
Littering carries stiff penalties
if you're caught. And there's
a tattered army on the roads
exercising total defence
against profligate nature
and slobs like you.

Offshore, there's a scattering of
disorderly traffic that we have
to tolerate, but Boy Scouts
scour our beaches, impounding
any foreign excess.

The rewards of prosperity must
be deployed with care, however.
Do not discard things thoughtlessly:
last year's steam iron, your
obsolete TV, that outmoded lounge
ought not be deposited
outside your window, dropped
from the balcony. The result
is unsightly, antisocial and,
from three storeys and above,
downright dangerous.

                        Do not
squander your emotions
just to see something fly,
to project into air beyond and feel
unrestricted experience of space.

Be warned:
your body out of bounds
may constitute offence
under the littering act.

Old Lag

1986

Since the island was too big to tame,
he settled down for the duration,
satisfied with basic comforts and a backyard.

Man Friday was shot on sight,
poisoned with indigestible gifts,
ignored as much as possible.

Reverting to his old pilfering,
he sold off hot rocks at cool prices,
a few forests, fleecing stray merchants.

Any solace of Providence was stuck between
brick and book-leather, frittered away
in sunlight, dust and drab amusements.

Refusing to admit the presence of many
other castaways summoned over time
by the smoke from a hundred easy prospects,

he no longer gazes at the horizon.
The occasional sideways flick of eye shows
only a dreaming outline of conviction.

Ulysses returned
1986

i

And here I am again, maudlin
with booze and feeling
absence of one of you
straining all my thoughts,
nakedness seeping to the night
breezes, just waiting
for dissipation. Wanting.

ii

Caught between spiders
and sexist webs,
we got the story wrong:
you never sat there,
craft and beauty
spinning calculations
until we were marooned
in each other's arms.

Well, perhaps you did.
But it was I, at least
reached out, fascinated
by you and cheating
archetypes – the
adolescent male again
devouring you in
consummate emotion,
instantly blind
to loneliness before
and after.

iii

Divide me, then.
Penelope, you get the familiar
restlessly domesticated breadwinner
at long last,
no more a hero,
slightly cowed by debts
of loyalty and admiration, owing
the children some stability
and school fees.
                        Circe, your charms
have made a grander second self,
the one posterity might with luck remember,
concocted of brash hardihood, chance
meetings and the moment's needs.
One of me is sane, ageing and careful;
the other always young, my own model
for resisting weaknesses, life's tawdry drift.
        Yes, I know it's not much
consolation, the division
is spoiled and you'd
both prefer it the other way round.
It leaves me
in a pretty sorry state as well.
This partial aftermath
of glorious all or nothing:
adventure's dreaming.

iv

Typically, Tennyson begged the hard question,
never saying if this crusty hero king got up
a veteran's reunion Mediterranean cruise,
ending it all in a rising rhetorical flourish.
Just as well, I guess. I know Telemachus
wouldn't be too pleased
left to keep the peace
again; and I'm not sure his dad
really relishes turning up once more
on the doorstep of a dozen or so
deserted wives and mistresses armed
with years of bitter spells and
assorted offspring claiming patrimony.
In fact, in these hack trades
of heroics and poetry
I'm getting tired
of discovering myself
at every port of call
just one more bastard.

Angry every day
1986

Fed up moving
on, keeping off;
fed up talking
another tongue;
fed up drinking
salt, dust and cheap booze;
fed up waiting
for someone else to choose;
fed up with living
under the gun;
fed up being
a second-grade slave;
fed to the teeth
with this struggle
to be fed
enough –
angry every day.

Displacement

for Gil 1986

i

'Grandpa Crayfish' – that's what
my daughter called you, childishly
slurring a suburb. (No,
not even that; too settled
for you – even 'village' is
wrong. Just an Institute and
tennis courts, a church, some shops,
a pub, and houses scattered
from one side of a valley
and across. Nothing tidy,
never quite a town.)

She was right, you know, you were
impossibly self-contained,
ensconced in this habitat.
Your shell (place, history, skin)
became thicker with each year,
more lived-in, impressively
festooned, motley, barnacled.

Not exactly a hermit,
yourself, your retreat never
completely isolated.
But how long do you think you'll last
when you're with all those others
waving their claws and feelers
behind brick veneer and glass?

ii

The starry-eyed young housemaid from England
that you conned out of the rich summer homes
amiably to fret away a lifetime
slaving for your orphaned brood, her short-lived
but tediously prolonged bedridden son
(What mutual passions, what disappointments
rankled? You never let on, that's for sure!)
she's now slouched heavily in an armchair,
bent fingers battling bravely with handicrafts,
legs swelling. She's happy, having married
her daughter to rich men so she can live
vicariously the life she'd only glimpsed
through kitchen doors, in magazines. Her world
now sedentary, is portable, attached
to memory, letters, photos, affections.
She'll like the companionship, the comforts
of a home.

                But in your case, I can't think
what arithmetic reduced you to this
decision. Your life had always been defined
in the cast-off objects of crude action
and a clutter of animals all housed
around you. Which of these will you take away,
what will be taken? The leather wrist strap
for the hand almost cut off when you went
drilling for water (I was seven then,
can remember the summer they brought you
down to Salisbury hospital, your brother

and those big nephews sitting way up high
in a clapped-out blitz buggy from the war,
all looming out of the sun by our wild
lawn, the tin house at the dry edge of town);
the plaited leather stockwhip like a snake,
old butcher's knives, big whetstone green with moss,
ox yokes, bullock shoes, a two-man pit saw
like an ancient instrument of torture
with teeth the colour of dried blood; what else? –
the bridle, stiff, black and cracked, from the horse
you put me on when I was four or so:
(it felt as if I'd never been so high,
seen so far so fearfully from your hill);
ribbons for the prize kelpies you once bred
(those lean brown silent dogs whose sniffing I
was never sure of when I visited,
especially the 'blue heelers');
mauls, awls, wedges, sledges, fence post augers
like corkscrews from a wino's wildest dream,
axe heads, a slug gun – all the mysteries of
your sheds.
     Multiplicity divided,
where will they go, what has or will become
of the kangaroos, koalas, lizards,
the galah that danced by the back door and
could take your finger off at the first joint,
the budgies, finches, guinea pigs, the chooks,
the homing pigeons, cats, ducks, the rabbits,
the stinking ferrets, goats – not to mention

assorted vegetables and fruit trees? Such
disorderly profusion made of you
a singular identity.
                How much
diminution can we bear before there's
nothing remaining to carry over?
Your sum total was a place; subtract that
and what's left? What's it worth to you to be
the best ninety-five-year-old tea-maker
in Uraidla? What's it cost Gil? Tell me.

iii

Amongst the 'incunabulae' to be picked up
by a sharp dealer for a song (the junk you
hoped to offload to supplement a pension)
my father found the doorstep to the district's
original hotel.
                But you never had
respect for institutions, wouldn't pass it on
to a museum or anything: 'Nah, Rex, to
any other clown it's just a marble slab.'

Keeping functional was always high on the list
of whatever you lived by – some set of
no-nonsense, unvoiced principles tied up in
pride and being busy, mastering a trade
and tinkering at a dozen others, never
completely content, not satisfied with youngsters'
efforts to emulate or help.
                      Something

of a doorstep yourself: plain, serviceable,
yielding only with a grudge to polish and time,
now worn from use. Barely noticed by the passer-by,
the rich customer, friends equally taciturn
and unforthcoming, your presence nonetheless
quietly signified, even when marooned
up beside the new freeway and its offshoot,
surrounded by the rising flotsam of local history.

When you leave, another door will close behind you.
Dust will settle, walls sag, things lose their shape
and disappear mysteriously. Eventually people
will scarcely pause, noticing merely
another slab of marble among weeds.

From a distance, then, carve in these memories,
a dry tribute – nothing grand – just to say
the living took a rough shine of its own,
not easy, not beautiful, but it'll do.

A Sceptic's Credo
1986

I believe in the ultimate salvation
of irony, dry underminer.
In religious pursuit of the partial,
there is comfort for a doubting soul.

Irony vaunteth not itself,
is not proud, because it turns
long-sufferingly upon itself
and its disciples.

It is a roguish creed, since it
like poetry, affirmeth
nothing, therefore lieth not
and cannot be held
responsible.

Its saints are few, jails
full of heroes quietly dying;
but because of irony
the bastions of dogma must look
to their foundations.

Irony is an act of faith
that when the dust settles
something will remain.

Continuity
1987

In collective self's self-fascination
the cults of horse and crescent moon still stand
resurrected in every revelation.

Cave journeys into light's initiation,
fate's systems imagined in the cards, your hand,
show collective self's self-fascination.

Man's music is the constellation's;
with stones, groves, mandalas, it circles and
is resurrected in each new revelation.

What is the helix of mind's replication?
Strung metaphors by which we understand
our collective self's self-fascination.

All alchemies of the imagination,
all Christs and Vedas, paradises, damned,
are resurrected in each other's revelation.

Faith, self-contained in contemplation,
speaks in symbols (not some creed's demand)
of collective self's self-fascination
for resurrection's many revelations.

Critical Response
1987

I am looking at a facsimile: a twice-as-large, doubly black blow-up of a microfilmed newspaper review whose chalk-white shininess glosses faint pink to mauve – print on paper; images of beams of light projecting someone's ideas on someone else's impressions.

More lately it has provided the raw material – and the soul for her first novel.

I am looking at this row of letters glaring an opinion. I am seeing the paper object that called them into being: two hundred yellowish matt sheets and a more delicate typeface, its slender rectitude holding at bay the overwhelming menace of Asian politics…a small publisher; now out of print.

The characters are dull; the story lacks interest.

I am not seeing the page: I am seeing a sky of twenty years past – perhaps the same blank pinkish white-grey as the paper I am holding. Certainly the three pages – facsimile, book and mind – all project Indonesia, though differently. Mine is not the troubled dark of the novel being reviewed; right now it surges into the senses with the same intensity of a still dusk hour in Semarang. It summons up a mood not experienced since, save for a summer's evening in a Mildura back-yard: the same blankness of sky, the same powerful sense of lonely calm, of being walled in by space.

It is a story of exploitation and betrayal… The retreat from heat, dirt, poverty and cruelty leads to a return to one's own kind from an inability to cope. Solace comes from the familiar. This is not to imply that the familiar is better.

Now I am waiting for the page to disappear again – for that sudden, treacherous possession of the senses, for the same kite suspended in the chalk-pink silent sky.

What bird is that?
1987 Singapore

Frankly, I don't make much of Frost's diminished world –
his oven-bird, mowed orchises, his cords of spruce.
For starters, his northern state of snow's not mine,
and anyway, I'm not convinced it's so reduced.

Looking out the back I see some birds I know –
the mynah, a kingfisher of the local kind
(the blue one with the outsized beak and yellow flash).
Most I can't identify, can just describe:
the light grey wader jerking a white neck, or
the creature that knocks in dreams at three o'clock –
'night-jar's inadequate, too blandly universal;
a better term is 'tock-tock bird' but that's debased.
What name will conjure up the qualities
and constitute a spell to make me feel at home?

Knowing every kind of bird or tree outside
doesn't just delimit a locality;
specificities pin down, but multiply the world
with questions asked by each new cry, or leaf or word.

Portrait of the camel as Australian
1987

Redeemed from northern deserts by brokers
of colonial economics and
a few soldiers, you were marched off, shipped out,
sold as workhorse for cattle factories,
carter for the wool conglomerates.

A Gästarbeiter exiled, you padded along
slowly grumbling, looking down
your nose, on lurching quest for the square meal,
painfully proud to survive on the smell
of an oily waterhole.

                    Your children,
ran wild, you and they viewed with amazement,
indulgent scorn, or ignored, forgotten
till wilderness turned mangy, desperately rampant,
confirming everyone's worst suspicions.

Now you're taking ship again for other
deserts to run for the rich.

                    If you had
never existed, they'd have had to mount
a royal commission to invent you.

Fremantle Reading

1988

A white-fire sky, stiff masts
stark black wag slow
admonishments ('Thou fool…')

There's nothing full or rounded
in this garrison of shops –
a film-set of rich dreams
reduced to sand, stiff
feather-duster palms and
silhouettes everywhere.

Nothing echoes,
least of all the words
that strive to dignify
a décor from Miami Vice
and transubstantiate
the lobster thermidor.

Poetry is not an after-dinner speech:
not here at the edge of nothing
but plate glass, a wharf,
the invisible immensity of sea
and a white-fire sky.

Extrapolation

1988

Brought up polite and young, I was
mostly a pious model child;
my teenage years were calm because
I lacked the know-how to run wild.

When passion came for what I owed,
family, work mocked all intention;
raging floods did crack convention,
marriage – but it hardly showed.

Emotions, though, will not be caged
in habit, laboured, homely, numbing;
just now I've succeeded in becoming
angry, coarse and middle-aged.

Maybe I shall learn the trick
of slipping into shabby fashion,
sagely propped up on a stick
pecked by familiar birds of passion.

But that's poetry.

I take life's hint:
there's no disguise
that doesn't scratch,
no timely gift
that won't destroy.
Watch old eyes:
they glint with bitter joy.

An Investment
1989

Percy Bysshe's food for fishes.
But while he wrote, his daily groat
came from a friend – not even kith –
a stockbroker: one Horace Smith.

While Perce would bend and rise in thought
unyielding save to inspiration,
uncaring what or where the next day brought
him, Smith would calculate inflation.

To poesy the chorus;
bread, travel, pen and shirt –
Smith's sharing failed in none.

So here's to you, good Horace;
bird thou never wert,
but yet made room for one.

Crumbs from an Australian Table

(a mostly found poem)
1989

To build an introductory lecture, I devour the text,
find Hadgraft making dainty meals of early verse:

'The adjective resplendent is a metre-filling word.
It sounded good to Kendall and no doubt he put it in
to fit his time, along with wonderful, ineffable,
sublime, and in more modest vein, sunshiny. All
of these 'poetical': they fill the mouth, the line, presumably
the understanding.'

                         But not, presumably, the gut:
I find some library reader's bookmark runes:
no literary pabulum, just 'Plates, forks, spoons.'

Koha
1998

The writer's house has
spareness and light spaces,
no surface without
some art of association
and exchange, of
talismans, mementos,
aids to divination.

I am too long consumed by cutting back,
reductive compensation, guilts,
the spare economy
of avoidance.

Can one give a koha
to oneself? Well, this
could be in spirit
of gifts from many hands,
minds, hearts; it comes
from where Witi thinks to live,
from green water stones
of Keri's shoreline
in graceful shape
from Potiki's carver.

It hangs heavy
with a calling
to the land, of
carvings up
of history
here and there, its heft
weights debts
to those dead, dues
to the living.

This pendant swirl
a hook for thoughts
of friends, a point
of circulation open
to fragility, to the new,
a sign of interest
to be handed on.

And so this kind
of carving
word
token, my koha.

Idiom in Auckland

1998

Conversing with a stranger,
we paused at 'thus' –
my mind looked forward
to conclusion, but
ear forgot its place;
the matter was at hand,
any conclusion
mine
and lying
elsewhere.

St Francis Church, Cochin
(1503 Franciscan; 1776 Dutch; 1795 Anglican; 1949 Church of South India)
1998

Flopping free of the
blue tinted cool
onto hot sand,
they trust to collective
carapace, elbow through
the call, dart, tug
of predatory gulls
to sanctuary.

These busloads shuffle in
and genuflect,
to scuff off
footwear, scattered piles
an untidy reliquary.

Discalced, they mill and hum,
processing aimlessly cross
pews and aisles;
three tour guides speak in tongues
of history – English, Dutch –
give witness to salvation
of discovery and trade (not much
remains in Portuguese). The East
redeemed, Da Gama's bones
were transubstantiated
home to Europe; photos
show the mystery
of the roped-off floor:

how was it
mild Franciscans left their birds
to tend the tombstone
of a murderer?

But fortunes turned.
The honest Dutch rebuilt the church
a tall fort, rock solid,
buttressed, same style
as warehouses busily
mouldering downtown.
God's godown, then, for harvesting
of souls, each to be sorted
by regulations one to ten
crisply displayed in cold white lettering
beside the company creed
and plaques to defunct shareholders.

In the fickle trade of time
stocks fluctuated like the
Damoclean punkah bars that
fanned the faithful
(outside pagans winnowing their words
with each pull of a rope).
Translated gravestones
declare flatly that
'Here nothing lies';
the smooth impression of
your ancestors is all
you get. The cameras click.

I turn away
a surfeit,
and there – quite perfect
in its stillness, past
the crows' complaining
and a vendor's thin flute, just
a wall, pure white in morning
sun that cuts a sundial slant,
crisp black of shutter.
Such a bright blankness frames
a bowl of white begonias in
a darkened room, brooding,
the calm contemplative
all instantly,
utterly
itself.

Kanyakumari

1998

Forget the bird's-eye view;
from a bus window you can touch
gutters both sides of the street.

Pilgrims in beards and black
scarves, T-shirts, lungi, faces
frolic like ebullient crows.

I calculate the crush,
the odds of clawing free
hands in green water.

This is it, I think: another ferry load
drowned in a news footnote.
Will I become history?

The temple guard, ignoring signs
for silence, sidles over: 'This solid stone,
all carve one piece.' I nod and seek sunlight.

At Kanyakumari the wind toys
with the volume of tourist stalls
incessant gusts of filmi qawwal.

A few faithful at the intersection
string a banner, shout a litany
antiphonal communist demands.

Six cows, a dog and two pigs
pick their slow way home
across the guest-house garden.

Some comfort from the bustle
and the sounds; the space of a sea breeze
at dusk, the straggle of familiar weeds.

Waiting on the Governor, inside,
tailored captains sprawl, khaki
stomachs rounded with seniority.

A soldier guards an empty room
against the sky, his rifle
languid by the tall windows.

The guide looks apologetically at clouds
while bullying northerners demand
the sunset they paid for.

Private Tuition
1999

Come now; the sun has busied itself
elsewhere and a grey wind exhorts
some sheltered industry. It's time
to brush up that half-forgotten language.

First, the mouthing of each syllable: lip,
neck, ear. Something more substantive: breast,
belly; then tongue-twisting syntax, now
relax. The smooth declension of a thigh.

Try the active mood next and
conjugation; tense! Don't forget
to work on your articulation – when to
be definite is always the hardest bit, and
Oh! There you have it – fluid intercourse.
More exercise tomorrow. For today, it's done.

Brett and Jodi un-Donne

1999

What's this compass shit?
Don't fart-arse around in circles,
stick to the point:
there's nothing like a good fuck.

Next best thing to getting out.
Hit the piss with the guys,
rage a bit. Nice to have her
to come home to, but.

Well, I guess it's nice and all
–
that romantic poem stuff –
but, you know, he gets to
go
off and I'm here, stuck.

I could get the single
mum's
and bus to Bellingen;
all said and done,
the guy's a schmuck.

Separation Blues

1999

School holidays are over,
you've just dropped your youngest back,
and the taut string of relations
has suddenly gone slack

as you drive into the flatlands
where the grass is whitened gold
like the ashes from a smelting,
whispering stories still untold.

The scrub is all hunched over
and the fields are red and bare.
There's nothing for a harvest,
only summer winds out there.

The snakes of truckies' retreads
rear black as you drive by,
and the car is full of memories
that will bite until you die.

Road stretches to the skyline,
sky's a blank of faded blue;
the landscape asks no questions
and no answers come to you.

It's suspended animation,
you could slip right off the line
between the new love miles ahead
and your daughter miles behind;

but the tape deck keeps you tapping
and the mileposts hand out clues
to the mystery tour of living
the post-separation blues.

Overseas Conference

1999

The bells of Tübingen sign off the hours
in triplicate: one, more particular,
counts in quarters the ring of
coin and burgomeisters 'neath
the studded timbers of the Rathaus;
one sounds like a navvy whacking
a length of rail with a hammer
down by the old brick factory
walling in the river;
and the last, forever setting
a low tone, solemnifies the inevitable
nod to church and sepulchre.
In town the timbered walls
sway around corners
and a soft gray rain falls timelessly
sheening scalloped tiles on new roofs
like the skin of red carp stretched flat.
A red-faced man stomps into breakfast
in lederhosen. It all seems so quaint
and self-contained, like the etchings
in a gallery, like Slessor's poem
on Dürer's attic, but by the bridge
there's a window full of
didgeridoos and in the woods
a tepee; it's a global world,
and down the road the airport
looks on at Stuttgart's concrete and steel,

several layers beyond the window boxes
and provincial charm, a history,
many histories, endless eras
of flame and death and looting.
Tübingen got lucky, someone
knew a thinker and a poet, had
enjoyed their studies there. Perhaps
a uni education still has something
to commend it; it once saved a town.

Pucker up

2000

A baby's born pickled, creased and howling;
only later and briefly smoothed
by breast or bottle, coo and caress
into the universal chubby infant.

After that, we grab, walk, fall,
smiling, scowling at experience,
the cuts of fate: our scarred integument,
our wrinkles mark us who we are.

Roads of emotions map our face,
our skin a ledger of returns, debts paid,
until, mostly settled, we take to bed.

And there you are in rosewood and lace,
composed as a stony crusader.
You're free of wrinkles when you're dead.

At the Airport, Seattle

November 2001

Some burly gunman in blue
picks me out, impassive, for
the random check pre-boarding.
It's the sixth from six long
queues consecutive. Must be
my vain attempt at dignity –
the careful clipped and
whitening beard. Or perhaps
the curious surname – should
I shout, 'It's English!'
or refuse reaction, fear? I flash
my Aussie passport, grin: 'I thought
we were supposed to be
your allies? And those who check
my bag, all Filipinos,
wryly smile.

Another damn elegy

2002

A world away from both our homes,
conferencing catch-up:
'Didn't you hear?' The journal's editor
found hanged in a Waikiki hotel.

See me with expression
of pained surprise; like
the actor blown backwards
through the tenth-storey window,
shattered.

We met in half a year
of classrooms. I recall
the cool intelligence
a teacher might find
challenging, the sharp
good looks, understated,
black hair.

You'd been the gofer
for good journals, professors,
mostly male, mostly
white. Your name
not exactly in lights
but clearly signalled.

It spoke class, old
continental family with
island roots, and somewhere
the island took hold, revealed
a different life, of rock
and weeds and streams,
the taro patch and
your middle name:
Mahealani e –

Your new journal was great:
strong black and white with
down-to-'aina issues. O'iwi.
And now here is
the unedited text.
Taku tangi ko oe.

In the empty room
did you seek to lodge
death in the aloha
heartland? Anonymously?
Was it a sex thing that slipped,
a Mishima gig? Camus?
you and your lover
brackets on emptiness.
Should I think of you dying
with a smile?

You both hang there/ in my mind
like an unfinished quotation.
There may be thirteen ways
of looking at this darkness,
but I am still stunned.
Dammit, Darlene: why?

the long-term car park
2004

sends metal feelers to the sun;
spread emptily over acres,
cars squat nose to nose
pugnaciously, a regiment
of baked cicada husks,
their contents flown.

We pupae stretch and crawl
and hum from shell to shell
to shell, each swarm a drift
desperate to swim, to run,
to fly so far, so fast
and free at last of aid,
of all protections, in that
one shrill transfiguration,
that brief burst of glory
as the season ends.

starting over
2004

Thrown together by a friend; shellshocked,
tentative, shuffling cutlery at the metal table
under a blessing of sun and the comfort
of public dalliance, we settle
for friendship and slow curiosity. But
with that heady zap of ozone maybe could turn
on give over to the current attraction.

I am intrigued by this
slow newness, a tentative regard;
how hesitantly we test the territory.
You slowly coming into focus,
a secret message feathering into view
in warming conversation. How strange
two so diversely travelled
to this moment can find
exchanges in the past –
a currency of grandparents, pianos,
the treadle Singer rising
black enamel, gilt filigree
like an idol on its shrine.
Books we have in common are
almost unremarkable by contrast.

You begin to fill the evening
with a richness of family, loves
for place and poetry until
the night curtains down and
I'm shocked to kiss
to hug goodbye, to feel you
actual body and
how small a frame
contains so much. This
careful gentleness.

Gold room #3, Hakoah Club

2004

They would get together to keep score
of kids, each other's fortunes, dance,
play cards and cry joyously 'To life!'
The boys lined the walls around
the starred carpet, Aaron's mob
hogging the stage as usual,
Gad hanging over the bar.
The twelve had joined
to form a football club,
had run across the rocks
and sands of Sydney's dreaming.
Their past now cupped in silver,
present promise is of gold
from a 'King of the Nile' pokie.
In his own Egypt, an old man
bowed down by Sunday suit and tie
punches away at his cowboy fate,
a 'Drifter' immobilised by age,
excess of leisure, absence;
and where now is the fire,
the cloud for this tabernacle?

Conferencing, Hyderabad

2004

There's always something new: today's
the first I've had to say,
ushering the audience in
as chair of a session to begin
(first day's security gone lax),
'Sir, why are you carrying an axe?'

A moment's panic; I foresee
some bloody mayhem, media spree:
My god! a deshi activist
with English Lit. on his hit list;
disgruntled author with a hatchet
a critic's blow with blows to match it;
performance artist on a pledge
to give our craft a cutting edge.
Ah well! At conferences you always find
there's someone with an axe to grind.

This gentleman is most obliging:
parks his tool and is soon subsiding
into snores in the back row –
a gardener on tea-break. So
session speakers hack their way
through learning's thickets; we display
our logic-chopping skills
in question time that slowly spills
to dullness, till my mind cries 'Pax!'
and reaches for that fresh-honed axe.

Sonnet XXXX

2005

You old idealist! Impediments
admit themselves, willy nilly, and most
of us want more than the true minds thing,
though that's part of the buzz – admittedly.

Time suspended by blue-eyed laughter, wine,
her voice singing forth a wise woman's verse,
the sudden clasp of hands, soft press of thigh:
these overcome restraints, spark the current.

My mind's a hotel lobby, her shadow
on the sunlit wall. Impediments? Try
families, job commitments, twelve thousand miles!

I wash shirts, socks, to make her absence go,
learning to accept the past, not yearn for charms,
to trust the day to day – committedly.

Country, and Western
2005

I'm driving again – it's
Christmas; my pilgrimage to parents
tracks the skyline across plains
that shimmer promise of arrival.

Tractors built like semis
plow up dust clouds storeys high,
grey sheep and black cattle graze the stubble
from sorghum paddocks the size of dry suburbs.

Further out, the saltbush stretches clear
on every side. I remember you said,
'Flat is not my favourite.' Well,
you'd really hate it here.

But you'd love the flight of eagles
and the rolling line of cloud,
the wind that whips the world clean,
a line of emus stalking the fence-line.

It's a landscape where the mind goes
when it's sloughed off daily care
from city life; the routine of farm labour
seems a ritual meditation.

They say open skies mean freedom,
plains make you your own man;
but the space around me speaks
your absence; come here with me when you can.

while you sleep

2006

While you sleep
I get the shopping done,
clean out the cobwebbed laundry,
read the papers in the sun,
water the pot plants.

While you sleep
the Swans battle Essendon,
a government changes,
wattle dust drifts on the wind,
a whale is freed from nets.

While you sleep
blue wrens dance me through breakfast,
the ringneck doves bob and burble,
a black rabbit chews up my garden,
cockatoos swoop and klaxon each other,
lizards flicker to and fro on the steps,
camellias carpet the grass in pink satin,
lemons exude their green tang,
bright day eventually fades to starlight.

While you sleep
half a world away
through all of this
I dream of you.

In Anticipation

2006

After all our traded readings,
all the Rumi and the Yeats,
the songs and sighs and silences
of tape, phone, email, cards,
the novels of our different lives,
what reading will I bring to you
when we meet? An ode
to the sunlight you have pinned
to my kitchen window? Hymn
to the companions of your new solitude?
The epic ballad of our journeying
towards each other? A plain
couplet of my empty hands?

When we touch again
it will be gently, each
fearing the enchantment
of our tales will at that instant fade;
when we meet again
I shall need to hold you
to feel you flesh and bone
more real than any story,
as miraculous as any song.

Rumi to Shahms

2006

When the hill behind my house turns
to sea of grass, the waves afoam
with paspalum seed, I shed
my daily clothes and don a robe,
some rubber boots, a hat, commence
a meditation, Step by step I tread, a
petrol-powered monk, whipping
the world into shape. I am

Death with mechanical scythe
enacting the demise of self, of all
proverbial grass cut down, I am
Michael with the sword of judgement,
the simple terrorist reducing all
to calm uniformity of green, and
then I am the figure in the garden
tending the wilderness.

                I do not know
what prayer is, but I have learned to
pay attention to the moves from shade
and broadleaf, dandelion, dock to
an attempt at lawn by the stump
of a clothesline (a man did this: it's
a hundred yards uphill from laundry)
the dense clumps of kikuyu in the runnels,
old bricks left for drainage, the rock
that holds the hillside down, dry
flame tree leaves that crackle and

the constant attack of lantana.

As Saint Francis may have said
(and if he didn't, then the Buddha probably did),
the buena and the mala are all yerba,
all grass is weed, all weeds are grass,
it just depends on how you cultivate,
how you mow, and so I walk, attending
to the whine of the shortened cord, the
pulse of cutting in and out at thickets
so the spindle does not bind, the exact
kiss of right length and swing and texture, all
becoming one mindless flow to the
engine's 'ohhmm' until the walk
is at its end and everything is
washed clean by wind and silence.

My Tess, it is you brings me to these fancies;
How is it that this hillside once
was just an inconvenience, and now
is haunted by two horses, a ghost
of scuppernong, and your beloved soul?

Sequel
2006

And now my hands,
my heart, my arms,
ears, mouth and mind
are full of you,
what next? How can
you be so overwhelmingly
present and still
so far away? You are
a dream, the shape
of touch, a texture
of scents, my tongue
memorises all your
photographs; it is
not enough, not
nearly enough.
You are the all-
consuming object
of my love; made out
of one tea break, dinner,
ferry ride, a blissful week
of walks, hot sex and silences,
and yet I want a subject
in the present, long
for the future, once so
improbably fulfilled, again
to make poetry
from random sense and time,
so we might hold and hold and hold again
our passion and companionate joy.

Stone Poem

2006

To everything there is a season

Right now, it is crisp spring; the sky
bright amethyst cut and polished by wind.
A tinfoil confetti of pigeons wheels and glitters
in sunlight, gardens
are incandescent with azaleas.
We saunter on grey sand, feet etched
by wavelets crystal-tipped
rock sculptures embrace
our stunned gaiety.

A time to cast away stones

The man beside me
is older, has worries
about his weight,
the stones that mark his past.
But his laugh today
reflects the sun, is light itself.
I wonder if it's us, or if
that mossless shine is
just from careless rolling.

A time to gather stones together

I can see why she picks up stones:
they weight her bag so
she doesn't fly straight up,

like some kid on an aircastle
delightedly angelic, and
fuelled on pure enthusiasm.
'Don't collect what you can't carry,'
she says, wise as ever;
and I wonder what small cairns
of memory line her windowsill.

And a time for every purpose under heaven

So perhaps it's stones that balance us,
sediment our feelings, solidify fires
of molten sex to warm joy that shines
or just sits comfortable in the hand.
Stones sign the rocks to be avoided,
boundaries to be observed, with stones
we can build paths or hearth, fell
giants, track home through forest, drown
or keep an even keel. Beach stones are clean
of guilts and expectations; jostled
together, or singly beached and still,
they are just content to be
washed by waves and light and time.

You can learn a lot from stones: they tell
the ways we tread this earth.

The Rubbayyat of Max

2006

Max went socialising,
alone and idly free,
set sail through waves of faces,
drowned in a cup of tea.

The sea change wrought a miracle, his bones
turned adamant, brilliants were his eyes;
but heart had turned to water – strange southern tones
ensirened him, he flowed to them while holding to his ties.

Accused of fickle Deppths, he played piratical and pure;
the rationalist buccaneer of heart, learning
from messages across the seas that yearning
was illusion to which there was no cure.

Mild-mannered Blackheart sailing down the email, threatening doom,
on landfall softly ravished damsel from park bench to bed,
who then revisited demurely in abandon, in curves, in lace and red;
and now the riddle is: who is the ravished: who has captured whom?

A mug of wine, chocolates, nuts and raspberries
and Tess beside him in a host of bedrooms exotic, plain and drear;
Becalmed, besotted, bestridden and embarded:
Says Max – and where now are the cares of yesteryear?

Says Max, there are so many moments, planned and chance,
so many of his selves marked 'Not my Favourite';
but one hour with Tess, one touch, one word, one glance,
for each he asks a life in which to savour it.

After Rumi
2006

I took my misery for a walk beneath the stars,
and sitting on the silvered grass,
heard a myriad insects ringing out
creation's symphony.
                            What word
shall I sing now, Shahms?
What theme is stringing me
a new movement?

On not meeting the great poet
2007

Well, his relish for
buddies and booze
and women all seemed so
seventies, embarrassing to find
how the genius had ended up
thirty years on. Besides,
I was having my own crisis,
hip sudden knifing me
mid-stride, back
hunching around itself, stiff
ball of torment.
A suave poetry of massage
became this moment's
necessary taste, backed up
by messages
on buses and beside
the aged care home that
I could be ash for $800, twelve
with ceremony, and more
for the full burial. Enough
then, to forego a literary visit,
think lyric in a blue sky,
the sun, and a poem
of six paces
of ordinary walking
free of pain.

Secular landscape

2008 Balranald-Hay plain

This canvas of scuffed tan, grey and parched yellow
unrolls dead flat, nubbled with saltbush,
a pop-up fringe of scrub, all stretched tight to the horizon.

The only verticals thin windmill ribs,
their faded sunflower head long lost in storms,
a hologram of turning dust.

Trucks appear
as high-rise constructions;
a rush and shudder,
they dwindle to a
dot.

There are places if you get
out of your car you are
the tallest thing for miles around.
Just stand; in time
a hawk will roost,
or vast laterals
will pull you down
to hear an endless abrasion of earth.

The sheep station entrance
Pretends a Dantean 'Hell's Gate';
It's a joke: the devils here are dust,
votive offerings bottles
thrown aside, placating
no gods of drought or travel.

An unremitting blast of light
morphs the road to molten glass
and you drive forever
to an empty universe of sky.

Towing
2008

In gentler days of motoring
when new cars were signed as 'Running In'
to smoothe their gearing going slow,
breakdowns on ropes announced 'In Tow'.

Now you don't find that at all:
Flash tow-trucks fight to win your haul,
And everyone's on wheels it seems,
all trailing something of their dreams.

'Cross desert plains as dry as hell,
go yachts, canoes, boats, rowing shells.
Golf buggies, surfboards, also roam,
and pensioners with their entire home.

If what you have is too much trouble
It will all fit on a B-double:
sheep, cattle, horses, goats and pigs;
two halves of house on separate rigs,

The meta-mobile going far –
A bus drags bikes and back-up car!
It can be shifted, big or small
With petrol, chains and a tow-ball.

Compared to these I travel light
Nothing on top, the boot shut tight.
But that 'In Tow' sign in memory
Still tugs at what is trailing me –
A weight of loss, guilts, sometimes woe –
That sign could also read as 'Under Tow'.

Deb's place, Calcutta

2009

The street cats jump through window bars
they're all bleached sandy gray;
they patrol terrazzo tiles silently
indifferent to the lack of scraps
and leave without a glance –
just another daily routine
like the broom seller's call,
thin melody of morning
bhajans, slosh of washing drain,
the unending grunt of crows or the
conch blown to household gods, the horns
of taxis, a child's toy trumpet,
a passing protest march:
such a whirl of layered sounds and
movement thick with life.

In quiet alley sunlight
a pious dog leaves its offering
neatly on a brick, it steams its
fragrance to Lord Surya.

An old man bespectacled and swathed
in grey chuddar surveys the world; he sells
paan sachets and cigarettes from his alcove,
as still and placid as a plaster saint.

Slogans for Senators
2010

I

To echo the angsts
Of online chat groups
Is not to
Tell it like it is.

II

Having the courage
Of your convictions
Does not mean
Repeating one idea.

III

The electorate
Needs more than
The politicians
It deserves.

IV

Giving the punters
What they want
Is chip shop profit,
But country-
Running loss.

Nature
2011

There's a bird with
the voice of an old
smoker outside. It
cuts through the
insistent shriek
of lorikeets,
the ratchet of
wattlebirds, wheezing
a reminder
that all is not
beauty, that truth
will trump youth. But
the bird itself
is just doing
what it does, and
is no doubt content.

Nicosia by the wall

2012

Dust and closed shutters,
stone facades of khaki
and grey timbers
withered to sinew.
One light aglow
in an archway
and four chairs
suggest welcome
for wanderers benighted
at some desert khan.
A still scene fixed
by politics; the only
green a line of trees
rooting through ruins
in no man's land.

Two Sonnets for Syd

2012

Delhi

Jantar Mantar's a sonnet in stone: a
Calculated frenzy, grid, filigree
Of numbers, one set echoing another,
All tracking avatars: the ziggurat,
Stonehenge, a stick in the sand. You must know
All there is to know to build this system,
That then will make the magic from which fire
Stairways catch stars, stone cauldrons offer up
A map of what you knew and need to know.
Such finesse, that whole elegance of form
Contains nothing of complete symmetry!
(Tourist plaques a new critical lesson:
unhelpful obvious paraphrase leaves mystery;
the thing itself fires imagination.)

Salute

Before the fire of Kurukshetra, there's
An offering, and all troops fight better fed.
For us, you were yourself the offering,
And we were fed by all those hosts you mustered:
On page, in person, worlds came to our table,
Till lunchtime made a legend in the world.
Since then, we tend our own fires, scrape rations
To feed the new recruits, and hold a line
That moves through half a world at least, inspired
Still by what your life and writings teach:
Pythagoras and Hopkins, like the old
Masters and Desani, were never wrong:
The fire is the offering, we are offerings
To the fire. The burning is our song.

Night sweats
2013

For hours a mob of wild bush horses
have been agallop in my upper intestine.
The tablets I'm on to fix some reflux
are wrecking my digestion; perhaps
this is Derrida's pharmakon,
but I doubt it. On that count I need
some wiry kid to ride breakneck down my gullet
for a quick bit of mustering. No thanks!
No semi-literate teenager's getting at my insides,
even if Eden-Monaro does foretell the outcome.
Yeats liked his horses, and before his animals
all deserted him, leaving only toys and silence
he prescribed words alone as certain good.
But he never used Digelax. Let's face it,
poetry won't fix my guts. I'll just
have to ride it out.

Requiem
2014

Alone in the evening
silence, cluttered
emptiness, I
contemplate
my mobile,
still feeling
I should call
my parents
now
a year dead.
It's surprising
this urge survives,
given
we spoke intermittently
at long distance
and only on the weather,
pot plants,
and curtains.
Their address book
full of childhood echoes
and never met friends
successively scored through:
few to tell their leaving.
And now
my diary too
becomes a field
of flattened stalks,
names blown who knows where
that whisper: 'Don't call us,
we'll call you.'

Epitaph for Chas

2015

The terrible grief of being human! Let
Us drink it all, but with a difference.
– Jalal-ud-din Rumi

In war things have to be precise
or you're dead; the line is clear.
But what more accident-prone than war? –
the mess of jungle firefight, the tangle
of guts and blood mire afterwards,
only some triaged for salvage
by jumpy half-trained medics.

It's only later that you've time to think
and confusion blurs what should be crystal.
Passion for things being just so
breeds disappointment, guilt for failings,
rage at complacent home,
its slackness, scorn of your demanding
exactitude. Only that last work writing
instruction manuals seemed to satisfy.

But you were up against it still:
the sly nature of language, stupid
users of the system. You took escape
in ambo action dramas, hustling
boy scouts into bush-walks, rigours
of survival, fads of exercise.

Action masked a lot, burnt only part away, caring
much too much, you never found it:
that peace in stillness.
Hit with one more conflict when
you thought you'd planned perfection,
some pyre of passionate sacrifice
was last resistance,
self-cauterised; you went
missing in action.

Perhaps that calm beyond desire,
past fear and time,
can now be yours,
and later, ours,
now that determined
desperate deed
ends all your battles.

DOA
2015

Whatever the figurings
of makers and muse,
most poems meet
with accident.

Their bodies lie,
left to crowds
indifferently boggling.

All poems look dead
on arrival, need
zapping to life
by teams of
compassionate
attendants.

To the Makers
2016

Songmen chipped and ground
their words to edge the law,
shape land to story. Law and land
both change and stay;
the songs go on.

The tinker sang his joy
at tinkering from door to door
till factory pots destroyed
his trade. But still
we sing his songs.

Songs praised the prowess
of weavers as the mills
took women and
their work away. But still
their tunes are sung.

This country's built on ballads
of poachers, bandits, rebels,
old prisons now long gone.
So take the tools of trade
and write your song.

Views from home
2016

1 Bedroom

In uniform grey,
rain sweeps the stage,
mopping up mountains,
trees, the town.
The curtain shears down.

2 Study

The Friday ladies,
parkaed blue and red,
a golfers' mushroom circle
of buggy umbrellas –
a Hiroshige woodcut.

3 Kitchen

Wind cuts away,
Sharpening all edges,
Filling shapes
With gunmetal wash.

In the evening trees,
flying foxes settle
shaking out
black pillowcases.

Amnesia/Scission

2021

Quiz show contestant, mid-twenties,
specialty: young adult adventure fantasy
with heroes (Apollo, Hercules, et cetera) returning
to (where else?) New York.
Asked one episode's original, replies,
'Oh I don't know much about those old myths.'

She's not alone. A restaurant, presumably not
wanting to reduce its customers
to tears, is called 'Niobe'; a jeweller
stamps pretty boxes with 'Pandora'.
What to do?

Mocking the ignorance, we can
bewail culture's decline,
but there's a touch
of innocence, a magic mutation,
in stripping tragic story
from old words.

Freed as happy-sounding
signs, they hint
a possibility:
that one day we
might see see 'ANZAC'
and think only 'biscuits'.

Developments
2022

Not exactly what we'd hoped
for, the block is cramped,
our gutters talk to next door
more than we do, no room
for trees. They say the land
was swamp and dairy
once, cleaned up by
coalwash and now no milk,
the road is cut and
water's rising.

Language lessons (lyrics for a ballad)
2022

The stone in the pocket, the board round the neck,
The dunce in the corner, they all put a check
On the talk in our schools, we all followed the rules,
And the words in our hearts bled away.

On a small western island known mainly for tin,
The people acquired all the words that came in
Till they gabbled pig Latin, Dutch, Danish and German,
Some Greek and more Norman, apart
From the tongues of the heart.

Then at some time or other, that creole turned mother
Tongue, sent out its brood on a mission to smother
The voices of people whose language was other
Than what was required to manage the world without bother.

The migloo, the gora, the pakeha, ang-mo,
So many masks for the privateer Anglo.
For after the conquests of Irish and Scot,
The Cornish and Welsh, they all joined in the plot
To plunder new places by using the ruse
Of offering gifts that you couldn't refuse.

The stone in the pocket, the board round the neck,
The dunce in the corner, they all put a check
On the talk in our schools, we all followed the rules,
And the words in our hearts bled away.

Though it's good and efficient that we all understand
What we say to each other from wherever we stand,
It's our histories, selves, families that live in the sounds
Of the voice in our hearts and the words of our lands.

www.ingramcontent.com/pod-product-compliance
Lightning Source LLC
Chambersburg PA
CBHW050611100526
44585CB00034B/1256